The Golden Age of Collectible Dolls

1946-1965

A. Glenn Mandeville

Published by Hobby House Press

Cumberland,
Maryland 21502

DEDICATION... This book is dedicated to the fond memories of my maternal grandmother and best friend, Ethel Hart Middleton, 1892-1986. Born into another world, she spent her entire life in her original homestead, built by her father, the village blacksmith. It was here in this old Victorian museum of a house that I learned the art of collecting and the joy of things from the past. Many a secret we shared, for hers was a love without conditions...the best kind of love there is.

Credits... Some very special people helped me on this project and without them, this work could not have been possible. To name a few, Teresa Carpinello, Aura "Gidget" Donnelly, Dick Tahsin as project coordinator, Bob Gantz, photographic assistance, Editor Donna H. Felger, Marge Meisinger and Dr. Victoria M. Hanfield who knew I could do it.

Note: The illustrations shown of real children are from old catalogs from companies out of business. Should any credits be omitted, the author will be happy to list them in future reprints.

Additional copies of this book may be purchased at $25.00
from
HOBBY HOUSE PRESS, INC.
900 Frederick Street
Cumberland, Maryland 21502
or from your favorite bookstore or dealer.
Please add $3.00 per copy postage.

ISBN: 0-87588-350-8

Childhood Memories
by Teresa Carpinello

My childhood years of the 50's
I know I could never forget.
Those memories are always vivid,
the years fly by, I regret!

Oh, how well I remember,
my childhood of carefree joys,
spending numerous hours of fun
with all of my special toys!

Of all my beautiful dolls, *Tiny Tears*
stands out in my mind, yours too, I'll bet
Saucy, Ginny and *Toni* Oh Yes! The *Revlons,*
how could I forget!

My sisters and I played make-believe
putting great effort in all we did,
thinking we were such wonderful moms
to all of our little "kids!"

We washed and ironed and set a fine table
for *Brother Coos* and our *Betsys.*
And after they ate we changed and bathed them,
Oh my, did they drink and *Wets'ey!*

On cold winter eves the coals would burn,
while watching our favorite shows,
like "Howdy," "Ozzie," "Sally" and "Froggy,"
And, of course, "Willie, the Worm!"

As I gaze upon my collection,
I lock my memories away.
But how worthwhile, I thought with a smile,
to have all those yesterdays!

Table of Contents

Ginny (1954) with her dog, *Sparky;* see page 101.

Sleeping Beauty by Madame Alexander (1959); see page 33.

Wendy Ann by Madame Alexander (1947); see page 18.

Part One...

The Luckiest Generation

The author in 1952, dressed like the perfect little gentleman.

"Never before so much for so few" *Life* magazine, 1954 describing the baby boom generation.

The years before 1946 were ones of survival. Like Europe, our country was in many ways a two-class society. The rich, no matter of what generation, had things that looked back on now seem wonderful such as the elaborate Victorian houses, resplendent with gingerbread, the victrolas, the love seats, i.e., the items that make the wealthy of any generation lucky. The poor, however, lived even in this nation of plenty in almost Dickensian poverty as the photographs of the late 1800s reveal in sepia tones of rural America drenched in nothingness.

So this trend continued throughout the decades of the early 20th century as World War I took an even greater toll on the lives of those that had not inherited nor exploited to gain "old" money and family fortune. The rich preyed off the poor and new industries such as Hollywood made a new type of millionaire, or *"nouveau riche"* of stars such as Mary Pickford, once the wealthiest woman in America, and her husband, Douglas Fairbanks. Together they built "Pickfair," the Camelot of its day and their life style became the standard against which the glory days of the flappers were measured.

Children during this time were often born out of ignorance of birth control or to be additional field hands. In fact, the "Waltons" image of a large, rural family was a reality-based fantasy as the more children one had, the more free field hands there were to till the field, yet consume little, for the farm was a self-contained unit whose solitude was broken only by the occasional trip to the country or general store where a piece of penny candy sufficed until Christmas when the necessary gifts of new shoes to replace old were exchanged.

In the 1920s, the illusion of fun existed in post World War I life, yet for children very little changed. Dressed as little adults from puberty on, they matured very quickly in order to earn a living or snare a husband.

Finally, the stock market crash of 1929 and the resulting economic chaos heralded a bleak time in which to be alive. This was rapidly followed by the threat of another global war, with a maniac at the helm in Germany whose atrocities toward humanity could eventually no longer be ignored.

Actually, it was World War II that spawned the great bulk of the population now known as "Middle America," for it was the ordinary man, in the guise of "GI Joe," and the common woman, exemplified as "Rosie, the Riveter" that made heroes out of the ordinary. Suddenly, the very rich seemed vulgar and self-centered. Millions were suffering world wide and with the bombing of Pearl Harbor that fateful day, another continent was

Friends magazine in the late 1940s showed the "Natalie Wood" child image. Note the Madame Alexander *Margaret O'Brien* doll in the window!

Howdy Doody and Buffalo Bob brought happiness to millions of baby boomer children daily on early television. *Movie Star News Photograph.*

The Cleaver family on "Leave It to Beaver" were the "American Dream" family. *Movie Star News Photograph.*

Millions of households watched the Nelsons grow up weekly on "Ozzie and Harriet." *Movie Star News Photograph.*

brought into the conflict and the common fighting man became the new hero of the newsreels and "flashes" of the commentators.

During the Depression, the gossip columns about the stars kept a nation from being depressed mentally but in the war years, a new hero emerged from the trenches...the American GI.

Morals changed tremendously during this period as the "pinups" of stars such as Betty Grable, Lana Turner and Rita Hayworth graced the footlockers of our fighting men. What would have been considered pornographic only a decade before was now acceptable if it helped a poor GI through this rough time. It was only natural that when the job was done and the war was won, that the new hero of the mid 1940s would be the American fighting man and his faithful bride waiting on the dock for his confetti strewn arrival back to a different America.

And different it was and would be for the fates had come together to create a time that never before was and never will be again. The baby boom was about to begin. Soon children would be on a pedestal, never before imagined, as the new middle class claimed a piece of the American pie now called the "American Dream," for a new dawn was breaking.

During the war years, technology moved by leaps and bounds. Energy could be devoted to making the returning GI a hero. Tract houses sprung up in suburbia. Modern appliances, credit cards, lawn mowers and cars became sportier and sleeker as a life style evolved that was as much a fantasy as a Disney cartoon. Yet who could blame Americans, long war and depression weary, from losing themselves in a Disney type of life. The description of the decade was one of a two-child family, preferably a boy and a girl, living in a

As this unidentified photograph shows, the little girl was the princess of the family. The dolls are by Madame Alexander.

lovely, manicured suburban home with a white picket fence. Mother always looked stunning, thanks to the new home permanents and "miracle" fibers that required no ironing. Father, in his spare time, tinkered with the barbeque, the lawn and romped with the kids and the dog. Indeed, the children were the key to this whole scenario as they washed across America like waves on the ocean, filling suburban homes and schools with apple pie fed, rosy cheeked, Norman Rockwell-looking little darlings that were, indeed, the apple of Daddy's war-stained eyes.

With the arrival of television, the news of the new affordable appliances, cosmetics, cars and other accoutrements of the day now reached into the homes of suburbia.

A lovely life style developed, helped along by the early television shows of the day. The carefree bachelor depicted on "Love That Bob," and the wisdom of inlaws on "December Bride" showed what life could be like in black and white perfection.

As the "family" shows arrived such as "Ozzie and Harriet," "The Burns and Allen Show," "Father Knows Best" and "The Donna Reed Show," television allowed a nation to set its standards by the manners and morals of the Nelsons, the Cleavers, the Stones and the other families of the day. Indeed, while looking like it all just "happened," as much care went into making a scene perfect as does on "Dynasty" today. Yet today, more sophisticated and able to see the reality in the glamour, the early shows were taken as standards that MUST be lived up to, or one was not fulfilling the "American Dream" properly. Unfortunately, many never could qualify for the "Dream" itself as black rural poverty rapidly transformed into black urban poverty. In fact, the unspoken hero of the day was the WASP (White Anglo Saxon Protestant), and to even be labeled as Italian, Polish, Jewish or even Irish often left one on the fringes of "Dreamland."

Even the "Mickey Mouse Club" was affected as Walt Disney allowed the charming Annette Funicello to keep her Italian heritage as an example of the new tokenism, yet made Don Grady (Robbie on "My Three Sons") change "Di Agrati" to something more pronounceable, despite his father being credited as one of the creative forces of the 1959 classic, *Sleeping Beauty*. In fact, to be blonde, blue-eyed and beautiful like the Princess Aurora virtually guaranteed success in anything from marriage to just admiration.

The suburbs rapidly evolved as the hub of the universe. Large, formal department stores began to open "branch" stores to service the new emerg-

An abundant, yet joyful baby boom Christmas in 1955 with all that a child could want.

ing middle class and ballet schools and little leagues changed the face of many an open acre to accommodate the free time that this new generation now had. Out of this time evolved the life style of the teenagers, who once only had washtubs and war uniforms to look forward to, but now had the money, the freedom and the time to develop a wonderful culture all their own, for there was now no reason to hurry along the process of growing up. In practice, children were kept children longer than ever before. Dolls and toys continued until youngsters reached about 14; then gradually the world of teendom opened for them, with poodle skirts, sock hops, pizza parlors and soda shoppes, all designed to make happy the little princesses and princes of the day.

It was more than money in the heyday of the baby boom that made suburbia the heaven that it was. Many fathers earned very little, yet their children never reflected that for the status symbol of the day was PRIDE, the belief in oneself that somehow seems lost today as rude, obnoxious children boldly tell off adults and even more rude and sometimes violent teenagers seem bent on destroying everything nice including themselves. During those golden years of the late 1940s to the mid 1960s, disillusionment simply did not exist. A child was brought up to believe that if one followed the rules, i.e., did their homework, cleaned up their room, went to school and got good grades, then a wonderful life would be their reward. My generation was taught that life IS fair; the good are rewarded and the bad, well they got what they deserved.

Indeed, the crossing guard, the policeman, the teacher, the preacher, even the milkman was someone who always wore a smile and in turn, was treated with respect. Even the crass Ralph Cramdon of "The Honeymooners" seems to be more a victim of his own ineptitude rather than a pawn of a society that no longer rewards the just, but supports the laziness and slovenliness of citizens who sit back and live off those struggling to make ends meet.

More important to our story, however, are the children themselves and the role they played in the household. Never were children quite as revered as in the boom years. Most fathers, including my own, made sure their children were carefully shielded from all of life's unpleasantness. To this day I cannot tell you if we were rich or not because the standard of pride and the philosophy that the children came first prevented most of that generation from ever knowing exactly from whence they came. To myself, "Leave It to Beaver" is not funny at all; in fact, it is almost chilling to me to watch the reruns and see the naive way in which trust and authority went hand-in-hand. Things such as molestation, incest or cops on the take simply did not exist in the butterfly-laden gardens of suburbia. If the occasional crime was committed, the person was properly and severely delt with and all the children heard were whispers after the bedroom door closed for the night.

The baby boomers grew up in a fantasy, fed by parents eager to forget the past, a technology eager to feed their fantasies and an economic climate of endless growth and prosperity.

Industries aimed this new technology at consumers and television brought it to the customer. The doll and toy industry was at its peak. The post war advances such as plastics and miracle fibers allowed the manufacturer to change lines yearly as doll wigs gave way to rooted hair and clothing became wash-and-wear.

The playthings of the boom children are today held up as the standard to which all new items are compared. It has only been recently as the boom

"SINCERELY" FROM
Fabian or Frankie

Toss Pillow and Photograph
Autographed For You By The Stars

YOUR CHOICE 1.98

FOR YOUR VERY OWN—FRANKIE AVALON AND FABIAN. What a sensation! Dreamy singing stars every teen is wild about. Now yours—to have and to hold—on romantic cuddlesome dream pillows. Personally autographed portrait printed on each pillow ... and an exciting, autographed 5x7-inch glossy Hollywood photograph too! Be the first to give or to own these thrilling autographed treasures no real fan could be without.

Linen-look rayon covers zip off for washing; use as pajama case too. Lining turn filled with bouncy cotton napper. Glamorous movie colors. Frankie green; Fabian gold or flamingo, each with White top.
79 J 1904 Frankie Avalon Pillow and Photo State color. (2 lbs.) 1.98
78 J 1905 Fabian Pillow and Photo State color. (2 lbs.) 1.98

The teenager of the household lived in a dream world of record hops and teen idols as this illustration shows.

children have grown up and demanded a return to those thrilling days of yesteryear's quality that dolls and toys are once again becoming close to what they once were.

We, who grew up then, are indeed fortunate in many ways. We knew nothing of what was ahead and, in many ways, that left us unprepared to deal with the unpleasantness of some of the present; yet we at least, for a short while, knew Camelot, which ended with the death of President Kennedy and the departure of Jacqueline. With it, life changed drastically as many knew the "American Dream" was often just that...a dream.

Yet to those of us who spent our youth in ignorant innocence, our childhoods remain as the most precious memories we carry, hence, our interest in acquiring, preserving and collecting the dolls and toys that we knew and loved. When we today look at a *Sweet Sue,* a *Toni* or a *Revlon* doll, or the *Lionel* trains, robots and cars, we are forever reminded that despite the stresses of the day, there was once a time when all at least seemed perfect.

Perhaps the parent of today, who is the bearer of these fond memories, will hopefully instill in their children that same sense of security and fantasy, yet mix it with enough reality for them to survive in the new competitive age we now live in.

For us baby boomers, our lives then were like a magic carpet ride...a journey we want to preserve forever in the objects we collect that reflect our rose-colored vision of living the "American Dream."

By the mid 1960s, the tranquility of the boom years would be over. Believe it or not, this is the author in 1964, complete with Beatle wig, "poor boy" cap and guitar!

Sweet Sue is a registered trademark of the American Character Doll Corp.
Toni is a registered trademark of The Gillette Co.
Revlon is a registered trademark of Revlon, Inc.

Part Two

The Dolls of Your Life

No generation in history was ever the recipient of more changes in their dolls annually than the boom children. In the late 1940s manufacturers were looking for a new medium to replace composition, the main material of doll manufacturing since the 1920s and in some cases before. Being a wood pulp base product (composed of sawdust, wood scraps and glue), it was subject to contracting and expanding depending on the weather, mainly the humidity. This in itself would not be particularly significant, except the dolls had to be painted over the composition and just like any paint on a wooden surface, the paint did not expand and contract, but gradually split as the material underneath reacted to the environment. Once a paint split occurred, moisture could get into the actual composition itself, causing severe cracking, peeling and splitting. Often this happened while dolls were in transit and it had been a major problem for companies for years.

During World War II a new synthetic material called plastic had been developed and was mainly useful for airplane parts. It was washable, paintable, moldable and just right in weight for many purposes. It was the miracle invention of the century.

In 1947 and 1948 doll companies began to discover this material. It was the most wonderful blessing in centuries! Molds did not even need to be changed as illustrated in the Madame Alexander catalog of 1947 which showed dolls made of composition and the very same dolls available in 1948 in the new hard plastic. Gradually new molds were developed for the liquid plastic was very easy to work with and results predictable.

Soon the hard plastic gave way to a new material called polyvinylchloride, or vinyl. Originally used for milk containers and other uses, it was perfect for parts of dolls because it had the feel and flexibility of real skin. It is still the main medium used today for mass-marketed dolls.

Mohair, the coat of a yak or other animal made lovely hair but when combed, thinned out until the wig was bare after just a few combings. Human hair was better, but supplies were tight and health regulations forbade its use on dolls beginning in the 1950s. American ingenuity came forth again with some miracle fibers such as Saran whose set was baked in, and nylon, which was the best of all fibers because it could be water-set by the child. Soon machines were developed that could sew the "hair" to a net base and be glued on a hard plastic doll. Eventually, when vinyl was used for doll heads in the later 1950s, these machines could root the hair right in the head, making a lifelike head of hair that defied detection from the real thing.

As technology from the war spilled over into the doll industry, other developments occurred such as plastic eyes that were lighter in weight and free from the shattering problems of glass eyes. The Vogue Doll Company

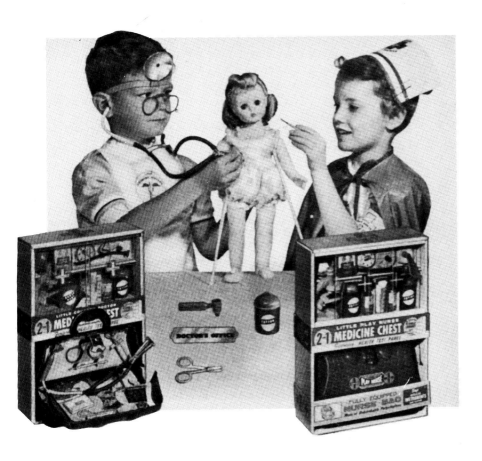

used surgical quality eyes made by the same manufacturer who made human replacement eyes! It was truly the era of quality.

Other changes during the boom years included walking mechanisms, talking devices, joints inside the vinyl that made legs look real when bent and a host of others.

When *Barbie* by Mattel arrived, so did the era of the extra wardrobe for a basic doll reach the pinnacle of success. While not a new concept, Mattel used *Barbie's* many activities to encourage her new owner to make sure she was properly dressed for every occasion.

In my opinion, the all-hard plastic doll made from around 1948 until 1955 is the true heart of the golden age of collectible dolls. These dolls are beautiful, with a look of quality about them not seen since the fine Jumeau dolls of the last century. Their place as a collectible that will only increase in value is virtually assured.

While all of this is interesting to us now as adults, as children all we knew was our dolls were breathtaking and that it was easy to talk Mom into buying them, for she herself had never seen such beautiful treasures.

This section of the book is designed to be just for fun...a trip down memory lane with some of the dolls of your life.

Barbie is a registered trademark of Mattel, Inc.

Chapter One

The Magic of

Madame

Alexander

I n 1923 Beatrice Alexander Behrman began a doll making career that rapidly earned her the title "Madame of the Doll Industry," a name that has made her a household word among doll collectors. For decades, a pink and blue box has spelled magic to those who collect or admire her creations. What began as a hobby soon evolved into a full-time business that her husband and grandson managed. During the golden years of the 1950s and 1960s, her ever-changing yearly line of dolls were the finest dolls made in America and represented the standard by which all other dolls were judged. The company never had to advertise as most dolls were snatched up as soon as they arrived in the stores.

Recently the family-owned business changed hands; however, Madame's grandson, Bill Burnbaum, remains active at the helm while Madame, now in her 90s, still acts as consultant and attends many functions annually, representing the company that she made famous.

Madame Alexander's motto has been, "A Thing of Beauty is a Joy Forever," and this is clearly reflected in all of her lovely creations.

This stunning all-hard plastic *Wendy Ann* is unique in that she has a human hair wig. Perhaps extra expense was put into the doll because Wendy Ann was the name of Madame's granddaughter.

The registered trademarks, the trademarks and the copyrights appearing in italics within this chapter belong to the Alexander Doll Company, Inc.

Full length of the rare 18in (46cm) all-hard plastic *Wendy Ann*.

Using the same mold is this hard plastic *Margaret O'Brien* doll which dates from 1947 and was made in hard plastic one year only. She is the same size as *Wendy Ann*.

Some authorities claim this doll represents Arlene Dahl but the author has not seen material on this. Still, she is a beautiful example of doll making at its finest. *Private Collection. Photograph by Neal Foster.*

This gorgeous 14in (36cm) pair of *Prince Charming* and *Cinderella* from the late 1940s would be a welcome addition to any collection.

Doll companies often loaned parts to each other as this mint-in-box Madame Alexander *Alice in Wonderland* shows; her head is marked, "R&B"! This came from the original owner and was never tampered with.

give
the world's most
fun-to-own` dolls
created by
MADAME *Alexander*

You've never seen lovelier dolls. They'll walk right into your heart with their impish little girl ways. Your child will adore washing, combing and setting hair so real (patented, woven hair of finest quality Saran that's just like her own) and selecting clothes from the fabulous Madame Alexander fashion wardrobe.

For an expression of wide-eyed wonder, watch your child's face when she sees:

● **Madeline.** (as shown) Fully jointed at wrist, shoulder, hip and knee for pretty posing.

● Kate Smith's **Annabelle.** With the pixie look.

● **Rosebud.** Soft plastic baby with voice and moving eyes.

● **Maggie Walker.** Walks where you lead her.

● **Dryper* Baby Doll.** Let her drink, change her real Dryper* pantie pad insert.

*Trademark

and many other original Madame Alexander creations.. the finest dolls made in America. Send for **FREE STORY BOOKLETS** and name of store nearest you. **ALEXANDER DOLL COMPANY, Inc.,** 153 E. 24th St., New York 10, N.Y.

Fashion Academy Award Winner for 1951 and 1952.

Madeline was a charming doll aimed for the wealthy child. She was ball-jointed like antique dolls. This advertisement shows that Madame won the coveted Fashion Academy award for her work.

Madame Alexander loved the royal family and in the early 1950s, she made dolls representing Queen Elizabeth and Prince Phillip commemorating the Queen's coronation.

A 1952 *Madeline* mint-in-the-box.

In 1953 Madame Alexander introduced her line of 8in (20cm) dolls called *Alexander-Kins*. These dolls are still in production and have undergone many transitions over the years.

A wonderful illustration from an unknown magazine highlights these beautiful dolls.

The popularity of these little folks even spilled over into Christmas cards. *Marge Meisinger Collection.*

A rare *Peter Pan Quiz-Kin*. These dolls featured two buttons on their backs so they could shake their heads "yes" or "no."

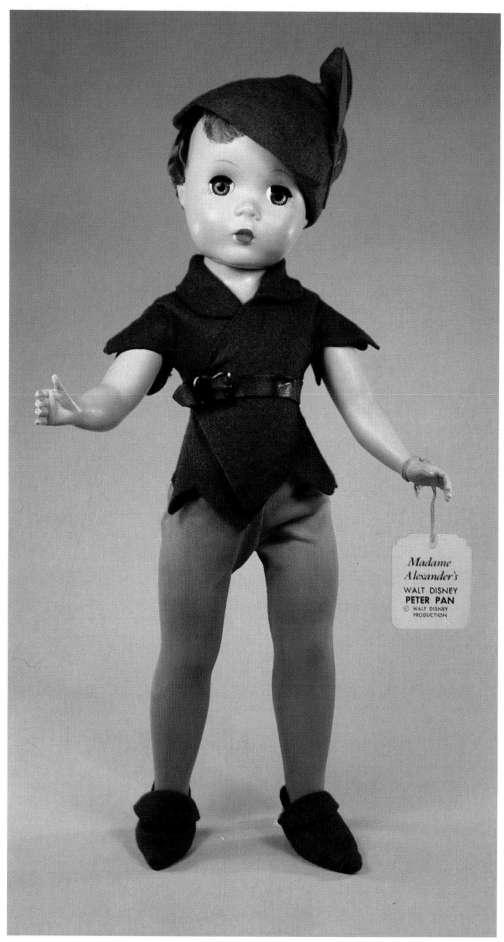

Madame
Alexander's
WALT DISNEY
PETER PAN
© WALT DISNEY
PRODUCTION

A 14in (36cm) *Peter Pan* in all-hard plastic.

Kate Smith's *Annabelle* was the subject of several size dolls in the early 1950s.

A ravishing *Cissy* doll dressed as *The Lady in Red*.

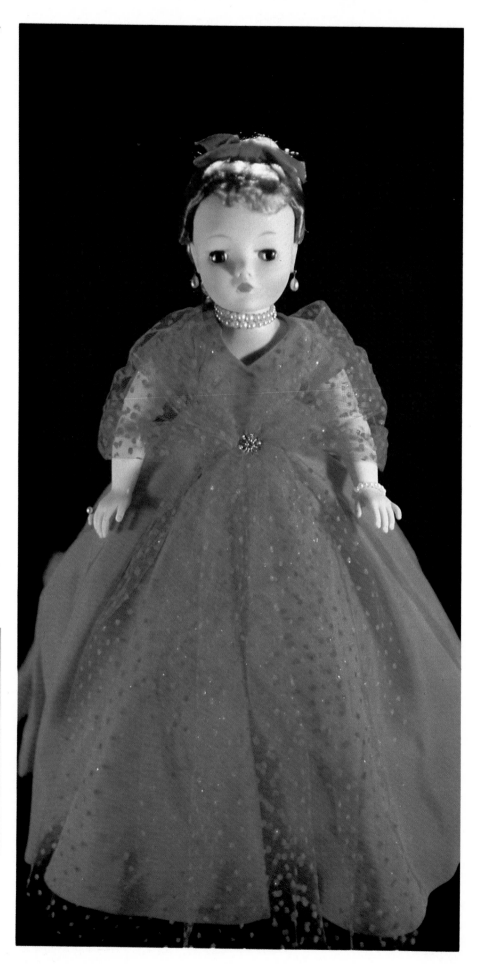

Yardley of London featured *Cissy* dolls in their toiletry advertisements.

Cissy was 21in (53cm) of adult sophistication as the baby boom children loved playing in the future world of glamour.

Two *Cissy* dolls dressed for tea, each with a chic hatbox bearing Madame's name.

In 1959 Madame Alexander joined forces with Walt Disney, making a 10in (25cm) *Sleeping Beauty*. For years the doll was believed to be a Disneyland exclusive; however, it was sold at Spiegel as well.

A portrait doll of Queen Elizabeth using the *Cissy* doll.

Vinyl came into its own in the late 1950s as shown in this 22in (53cm) *Kelly* and matching *Wendy* in hard plastic.

The same face was used on the 1960 *Pollyanna* doll.

One of the most charming dolls ever made by Madame Alexander was this 8in (20cm) *Maggie Mix-up* in 1960-1961. Today the company is again using this face on its dolls, much to the delight of collectors.

An early 1960s *Gibson Girl* in a 10in (25cm) size. This face has also been reissued and is again being used for dolls.

A 10in (25cm) *Jacqueline* was also available in the famous pillbox hat of the period.

A portrait doll in the 21in (53cm) size with a new vinyl face and named *Jacqueline*. No mention of the Kennedy name was attached. The doll wears an exact replica of Jacqueline Kennedy's inaugural ball gown.

A close-up of a stunning mint *Jacqueline*.

While just outside the boom years, I could not resist showing the fabulous 1966 *Coco*-faced *Renoir Portriat* doll. The mold was never used again and these are the diamonds of the Alexander dolls.

Also beyond the boom years, 1968, is the fabulous *Easter Doll* created in a limited edition of 320 dolls at the request of Frank Martin, West Coast representative for the Alexander Doll Company, Inc.

Chapter Two

Ideal...

Images of Children

The Ideal Toy Corporation dates back to 1902 and was founded by Morris Mitchtom to create his teddy bear. Over the years Ideal has produced some of the dolls collectors today are feverishly seeking. In the 1930s the company found fame with securing rights to the *Shirley Temple* doll which was reissued again in circa 1957 for the baby boom children which fell in love with Shirley, not in the movies, but on television. Their series of life-sized dolls, the *Playpals*, the size of three-year-old children, were the best known of the companion dolls of the early 1960s. While not often put on the pedestal that Madame Alexander dolls are, Ideal also made some of the most famous and creative of the baby boomer playthings.

This rare P-93 20in (51cm) *Toni*® represents the height of baby boom nostalgia. Made of the new all- hard plastic, she came with a *Toni*® home permanent kit and a nylon wig. She is the most famous doll of the 1950s.

A rare brunette 14in (36cm) *Toni* doll, mint as mint can be.

Toni is a registered trademark of The Gillette Co.

The original packaging for the *Toni* dolls. These boxes add to the value of the dolls because of the clever illustrations.

Original advertisement for the *Toni* doll that appeared in many catalogs.

Toni is a registered trademark of The Gillette Co.

Ideal even knocked off their own doll in *Sara Ann* that featured Saran hair instead of nylon and was minus the expensive Toni® license.

Toni® is a registered trademark of The Gillette Co.

Mary Hartline, the Pretty Princess of television, was captured in doll form in all-hard plastic using the *Toni* molds in the early 1950s.

Toni® is a registered trademark of The Gillette Co.

The end of the *Mary Hartline* box shows the startling resemblance despite the use of the ordinary mold.

Miss Curity was another doll to use the *Toni*® molds and came with a play nurse kit for the child.

Toni® is a registered trademark of The Gillette Co.

46

Close-up of *Miss Curity* showing
she is of the same mold!

Brother and *Baby Coos* were hard plastic headed dolls that delighted many a boom child. *Teresa Carpinello Collection.*

A vinyl version of the *Toni®* face was used on *Princess Mary* in the early 1950s.

Toni® is a registered trademark of The Gillette Co.

An advertisement showing the Bakelite hard plastic used on Ideal dolls.

McCalls magazine had a hit with Betsy McCall.® Ideal captured her in doll form with a hard plastic body, new vinyl head stuffed with cotton batting and featuring a glued-on wig.

Betsy McCall® is a registered trademark of the McCall Corp.

The *Revlon* doll was big sister to many a baby boomer little girl. The artwork portrayed the glorious future a child had to look forward to.

Featured with the 20in (51cm) *Revlon* doll is the rare 15in (38cm) version of the same doll. These dolls are almost impossible to find today.

A stunning close-up of a 1957 *Revlon* doll in a 20in (51cm) size. She is made of vinyl, the new miracle material of the late 1950s.

Revlon is a registered trademark of Revlon, Inc.

A 10in (25cm) *Little Miss Revlon®* was part of the line as well and featured several extra boxed outfits. She was a forerunner of the *Barbie®* doll.

A new generation had discovered Shirley Temple on television so Ideal issued several size dolls in vinyl with rooted hair such as this 19in (48cm) size.

Another rare size *Revlon®* doll is the 22in (56cm) size.

Revlon® is a registered trademark of Revlon, Inc.
Barbie® is a registered trademark of Mattel, Inc.

A deluxe version had "flirty eyes."

Close-up of the deluxe 17in (43cm) "flirty-eyed" *Shirley Temple.*

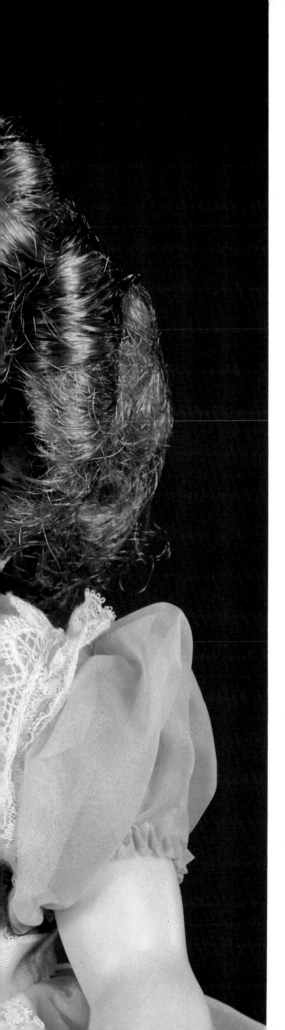

Also available in a great variety of outfits was a 12in (31cm) version of *Shirley Temple*.

"Companion" or life-size dolls were all the rage in the late 1950s and early 1960s. The most popular was this 36in (91cm) *Patti Playpal. Jan Amme Collection.*

Group shot of the *Playpal* dolls including American Character's *Sandy McCall* at the wheel! *Teresa Carpinello Collection.*

Outfits were available for these dolls depicting local celebrities such as this *Sally Starr* ensemble. Sally Starr was a local Philadelphia television personality. *Teresa Carpinello Collection.*

Patti Playpal also came in a smaller 15in (38cm) version called *Petite Patti. Teresa Carpinello Collection.*

Peter Playpal was aimed for both boys and girls and was quite lifelike. *Gidget Donnelly Collection.*

The younger member of the *Playpal* family was *Penny Playpal.* She was 32in (81cm) in height and extremely lifelike. *Gidget Donnelly Collection.*

61

Lori Martin starred in a remake of the Elizabeth Taylor classic *National Velvet* and was also a large doll by Ideal.

One of the large dolls in the early 1960s was *Miss Ideal*. She was jointed and of high quality. *Colleen Giles Collection.*

A close-up of a larger size *Miss Ideal.*

The *Tammy* series of dolls was Ideal's answer to *Barbie®* by Mattel. While more innocent, she only lasted a few years and had an entire family.

Capitalizing on the name "Jackie," which spelled magic in the early 1960s, Ideal issued their own fashion doll which today is quite difficult to find.

The *Flintstones* were the last of the boom dolls made by Ideal as the adorable *Pebbles* and *Bamm-Bamm* show here. *Teresa Carpinello Collection.*

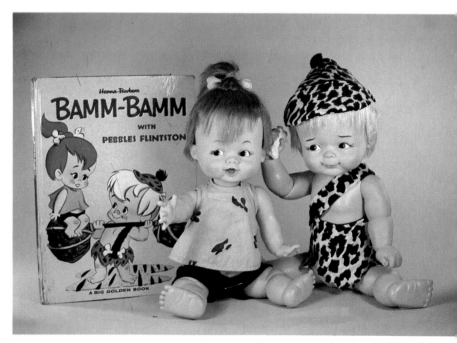

Remember—only you can PREVENT FOREST FIRES!

IDEAL'S
SMOKEY

THE FOREST
FIRE PREVENTIN
BEAR

SMOKEY

SMOKEY BEAR WANTS EVE
BOY AND GIRL TO B
JUNIOR FOREST RAI
AND
HELP PREVENT FORES

YOUR ENROLLMENT CARD IS IN

IT'S A WONDERFUL T

Ideal cannot be forgotten for its plush which started the company. This *Smokey* bear dates from the early 1950s and was for both boys and girls. *Teresa Carpinello Collection*.

Chapter Three

American Character...

Sweet Dreams

T he American Character Doll Corp. brought sweet dreams to many a child who longed for a quality doll. The company, formed in 1918, made some of the finest 1950s and 1960s dolls, until its demise in 1968.

The beautiful hard plastic *Sweet Sue* and vinyl *Toni* and *Betsy McCall* are just a few of the superbly manufactured dolls the company supplied little girls and collectors with. Fortunate for those who received such wonderful dolls and for those who did not, it left many with visions of these treasures in their dreams...their sweet dreams!

This 14in (36cm) *Toni* doll captures the teenage sophisticate look popular in the late 1950s. The doll is from 1959 and shows how *Toni* grew up with the boom children.

An early advertisement for the all-hard plastic *Sweet Sue* and her Charles of the Ritz chignon hair piece. *Marge Meisinger Collection.*

An 18in (46cm) *Sweet Sue* walker from around 1954 shows off her ball gown.

The all-hard plastic *Sweet Sue* dolls of the early 1950s were of the highest quality as this 20in (51cm) beauty shows.

A toddler *Sweet Sue* made of the new miracle plastic.

Sweet Sue was also available as *Alice in Wonderland* in the early 1950s.

Full length version of *Betsy McCall* as a schoolgirl.
Betsy McCall is a registered trademark of the McCall Corp.

A large 25in (64cm) size doll was also available and was all-hard plastic.

American Character took over the *Betsy McCall* license in the late 1950s and made a charming version shown here with *Betsy's* famous watermelon grin.

The *Toni*® doll also came in this demure 10in (25cm) size that competed with the *Little Miss Revlon*® doll by Ideal. Her vinyl was of high quality.

Sweet Sue Sophisticate was the vinyl grown-up version of the little girl, *Sweet Sue*, from the early 1950s.

Full view shot of the first illustration in this chapter with her hatbox and dress.

An all-hard plastic little 8in (20cm) *Betsy McCall®* was a very popular doll. She had over 100 extra outfits that could be purchased for her in the late 1950s and early 1960s.

Betsy McCall® Gift Sets included the doll plus an adventure theme.

Betsy McCall® is a registered trademark of the McCall Corp.

BETSY McCALL DESIGNERS STUDIO

Larger sizes were available of both
Toni and *Sweet Sue* which were ba-
sically the same doll. *Teresa Carpinello Collection.*

Toni° is a registered trademark of The Gillette Co.

Tressy with growing hair was American Character's answer to *Barbie®* but she did not make it as a commercial success.

Barbie® is a registered trademark of Mattel, Inc.

The Whimseys were an all-vinyl fun doll group of the early 1960s, the last of the American Character great dolls.

Chapter Four

The Magnificent

Mattel

T he "magnificent" Mattel toy company was founded in 1945 by Elliot and Ruth Handler and Harold Matson. The company name stemmed from "Matt," for Matson and "el" for Elliot and originally was primarily a doll house manufacturer. However, in 1947 the company found a toy hit with their Uke-A-Doodle, a musical toy. Soon after, Mattel became a sponsor on ABC-TV's "Mickey Mouse Club" where they showcased many of their new toys directly to their key audience — the children.

In 1959 *Barbie...Teen-Age Fashion Model* doll made her debut nationwide on the "Mickey Mouse Club" and was an immediate sensation with the children — they loved her! The rest, as they say, is history. *Barbie* was and still remains Mattel's and America's most popular doll. Mattel also found hits with their talking dolls, *Chatty Cathy, Matty Mattel, Sister Belle* and a host of others, truly making them the "magnificent" Mattel.

The face that launched a thousand dreams and made millions for Mattel, the 1959 debut look of *Barbie...Teen-Age Fashion Model*, wearing "Roman Holiday Separates."

A NRFB blonde #1 *Barbie*. Little did children and adults alike know that *Barbie* would quickly become the most popular doll of all time.

One of *Barbie's* earliest careers, besides being a top teenage fashion model, was as a fashion designer. A beautiful #3 brunette models *Busy Gal*, a chic fashion designer uniform complete with monogrammed black portfolio with garment sketches inside!

A lovely #4 brunette *Barbie* dressed in *Nighty Negligee* advertises her signature bubble bath.

Since her debut in 1959, *Barbie's* popularity has grown and grown. As a result, numerous licensed products with the *Barbie* trademark appeared on the market, ranging from rings to records. It has been evident that the name *Barbie* has not only meant fun and fantasy, but big bucks!

Barbie and her new boyfriend, *Ken*, play at being married and pose for a 1961 wedding snapshot. Today, nearly 30 years after their first date, *Barbie* and *Ken* still remain unwed!

Barbie's glamorous evening gowns were part of her signature from her inception. Here a #4 blonde ponytail *Barbie* models *Solo in the Spotlight* and a blonde bubble-cut *Barbie* models *Enchanted Evening*. Both ensembles are from 1960 and considered "*Barbie*" classics."

A rare version of a 1964 German Swirl *Barbie*, rare being that she came dressed in the striped *Fashion Queen* bathing suit rather than the usual red helanca swimsuit.

Barbie and *Ken* traveled to Mexico in 1964 and here show us their authentic south-of-the-border costumes.

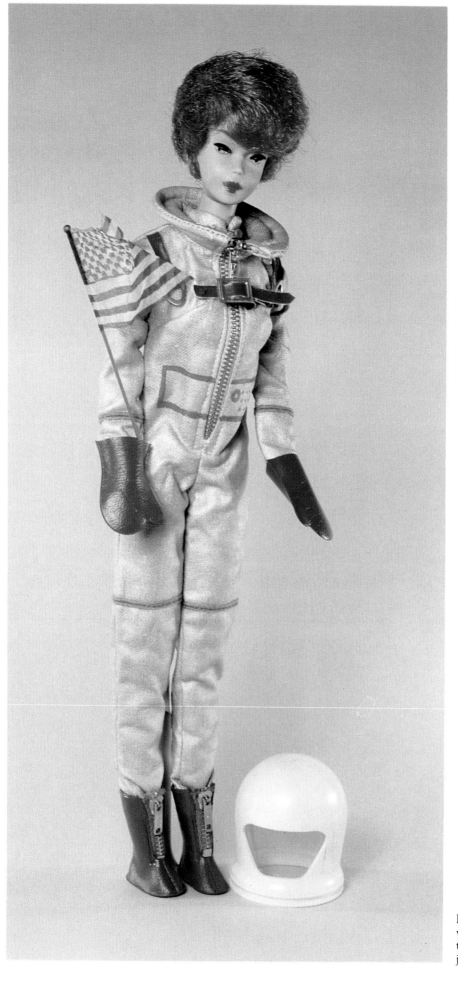

In 1965 *Barbie* traveled to the moon wearing *Miss Astronaut* and proved to America that she was more than just a pretty face!

The 1965 version of *Barbie* and her best friend, *Midge*, featured new bendable legs and new hairstyles. Here the duo step out in style with *Midge* wearing *International Fair* and *Barbie* wearing *Music Center Matinee*.

The adorable *Chatty Cathy* truly crafted upon the look of the early 1960s child, as she clearly shows here with her wide-eyed expression.

A pig-tailed *Chatty Cathy* poses with her original box.

MATTEL'S
Chatty
Cathy

I can say all these things!

Chatty Cathy
THE TALKING DOLL!

Sister Belle was another pull-string talking doll available in 1961. *Belle*, however, was not all-vinyl like the *Chatty* dolls. She sported a cloth body and plastic head as did her brother, *Matty Mattel*.

In 1961 *Tiny Chatty Baby Sister* and *Brother* appeared shown here dressed as twins, but outfits should be switched! The short-haired doll is the girl.

Chapter Five

Vogue Dolls...

Made With Love

T he Vogue Doll Shoppe opened its doors in 1922 under the able direction of Mrs. Jennie Graves, who began by sewing outstanding clothing for imported antique dolls from Germany. By 1951 she had made a name for herself in the miniature doll business and introduced the famous *Ginny* doll, named for her daughter, Virginia Graves Carlson. There have been many *Ginny* imitators but none quite as fetching as the little toddler that she represented. Over the years, the *Ginny* doll changed construction and the company changed hands several times. It is currently under the guidance of Dakin, Inc., in San Francisco.

This sensational *Ginny* doll named *Eve* is truly an American toddler doll.

The late 1940s saw the end of the composition dolls such as this *Fairy Godmother.*

The next transition for *Ginny* was this painted-eye version that was available from 1948 to 1950. She was made of the new miracle hard plastic.

As the miniature dolls evolved, many models had new features such as the sleep eyes introduced in 1951.

Steve and *Eve*, brother and sister, pose as the ultimate baby boomer dolls.

EVE
No. 36

Storybook characters were always loved by children as shown in the beautiful *Alice in Wonderland* from the early 1950s.

Another of the named sleep-eyed dolls, this is *Linda*.

A doll named *Wanda* shows the skill of Virginia Graves Carlson who designed *Ginny's* fantastic wardrobe. The doll was named for her, also, for she was Mrs. Graves' daughter.

A black version of *Ginny* was available in 1953 and 1954. It was not a big hit and so was rapidly discontinued. Today it is very difficult to locate and quite valuable.

Ginny showed little girls many career options never before depicted in doll form. Mrs. Graves felt little girls should have choices in life.

In 1954 Ginny could walk. Her dog, Sparky, was made by Steiff.

In the late 1950s *Ginny* had a teen-age sister, *Jill*, who was a typical teen of the day shown in her "record hop" skirt. Her companion is *Jeff*, another Vogue family member.

A later 1950s *Ginny* with bending knees with sister, *Jill*, in the kitchen. *Teresa Carpinello Collection.*

Ginny also had a baby sister, *Ginnette*, shown here ready for play in her very own pool set. *Teresa Carpinello Collection.*

Jill became a vinyl doll at the end of the boom years and these later dolls such as this *Jill*, dressed as a pilgrim, are quite difficult to find.

Chapter Six

Assorted Leading
Manufacturers

E ffanbee, Terri Lee, Mary Hoyer, Nancy Ann, Horsman, Royal and many more were other leading doll manufacturers of the 1950s and 1960s that produced high quality dolls for the luckiest generation. Some companies were more popular and prominent in some areas than others.

Dolls like the famous *Terri Lee,* *Little Lady* by Effanbee and *Nancy Ann Style Show* by Nancy Ann gave many a baby boomer child hours of fantasy and fun. Beauty and quality go hand-in-hand with these assorted leading manufacturers.

The rare beauty of this Effanbee *Honey* doll made in the early 1950s of all hard plastic with nylon hair cannot be put into words.

Honey is a registered trademark of the Effanbee Doll Company.
Terri Lee is a registered trademark of The Terri Lee Sales Corp.
Little Lady is a registered trademark of the Effanbee Doll Company.
Nancy Ann Style Show is a registered trademark of Nancy Ann Storybook Dolls, Inc.

The same all-hard plastic *Honey*[*] doll was dressed by Schiaparelli, the French designer, and marketed in America.

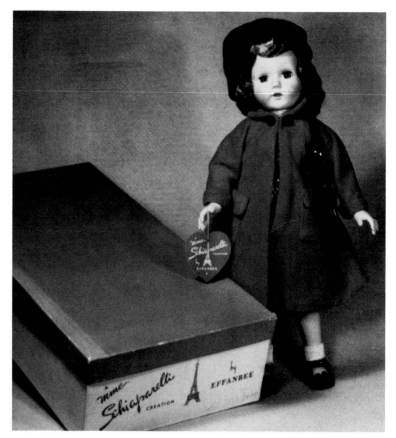

Effanbee and Madame Alexander were in fierce competition for the best dolls during the early boom years as shown in this pair of *Prince Charming*[*] and *Cinderella*[*] by Effanbee. *Robert Tonner Collection.*

Honey[*] is a registered trademark of the Effanbee Doll Company.
Prince Charming[*] and *Cinderella*[*] are registered trademarks of the Effanbee Doll Company.
Terri Lee[*] is a registered trademark of the Terri Lee Sales Corp.

The *Terri Lee* dolls were dolls you either adored or despised. Having a strange look, they were all-hard plastic and nearly indestructible. *Terri Lee*® is a registered trademark of the Terri Lee Sales Corp.

Here is the real Terri Lee® family
from which the dolls were modeled.

A mint *Terri Lee*® models a cheer-
leader outfit.

Terri Lee® and *Jerri Lee*® are registered trademarks of the Terri Lee Sales Corp.

A boy, *Jerri Lee*®, was also available.

Talking Terri Lee® was a clever invention whereby a record could be played through a speaker in the doll.

A black version of *Terri Lee®* was available for awhile but like other black dolls of the early 1950s, was not a financial success.

Terri Lee® and *Talking Terri Lee®* are registered trademarks of the Terri Lee Sales Corp.

The Mary Hoyer Doll Mfg. Co. of Reading, Pennsylvania, produced lovely dolls that were made to be dressed at home. *Teresa Carpinello Collection.*

This all-hard plastic beauty is a Horsman doll from the early 1950s. Horsman was a Trenton, New Jersey, based firm.

Horsman also made companion dolls such as this 36in (91cm) *Mary Poppins* under Disney license.

Horsman made vinyl dolls later on in the decade. This *Cindy®* doll looks like the hard plastic *Cissy®* doll by Madame Alexander.

Cindy® is a registered trademark of Horsman Dolls, Inc. *Cissy®* is a registered trademark of the Alexander Doll Co., Inc.

A smaller version of *Mary Poppins* was available in a gift set.

Saranade doll, manufacturer unknown, was another great boom doll. *Teresa Carpinello Collection.*

Wee Three® is a registered trademark of the Uneeda Doll Company, Inc.

The Uneeda Company captures family life in the late 1950s with *Wee Three* representing a mother and her children. Note the "movie star" blonde hair on Mom!

In 1963 Remco captured the ideal
American family in a set of dolls
called *The Littlechaps.*

Hasbro made this bizarre *Little Miss No Name* who was in desperate need of a name. Her box is wonderful and depicts the doll in a Dickens' setting behind a blizzard raging outside.

G.I. Joe, America's Fighting Man, was Hasbro's contribution to the growing interest little boys had in dolls. They were safely called "action figures."

Chapter Seven

The Other Dolls
We Loved

W hile many think of the boom years as reflecting the gorgeous display windows of the New York department stores filled with dolls by Madame Alexander and Ideal, there were many other manufacturers who made dolls that were available in Mom and Pop toy stores (virtually nonexistent today), hardware stores and even supermarkets. Most of these dolls were direct copies of the higher-priced dolls and were often done so well that a child could not tell the difference, especially the younger child who was not so label conscious.

Ironically, these dolls today are much more difficult to find mint or in any condition as they were not widely distributed and did not last long in the marketplace. Unfortunately, collectors often snub these dolls by lesser manufacturers as inferior when often they are not, as the illustrations here prove. For many a baby boomer, "generic" dolls were the ones they loved and lucky is the collector of this type of doll for most of these dolls can be found today "mint" for a fraction of what the same doll with a fancy name would cost. Do not neglect these dolls for they represent a slice of Americana that many remember dearly.

The lovely *Lu Ann Simms* from Arthur Godfrey's television show. Produced by the Valentine Co., this hard plastic doll is truly a treasure!

One of
Arthur Godfrey's
friends
LU ANN
Simms
WALKING
DOLL
CBS TELEVISION STAR
MFG. BY
ROBERTA DOLL CO., INC.

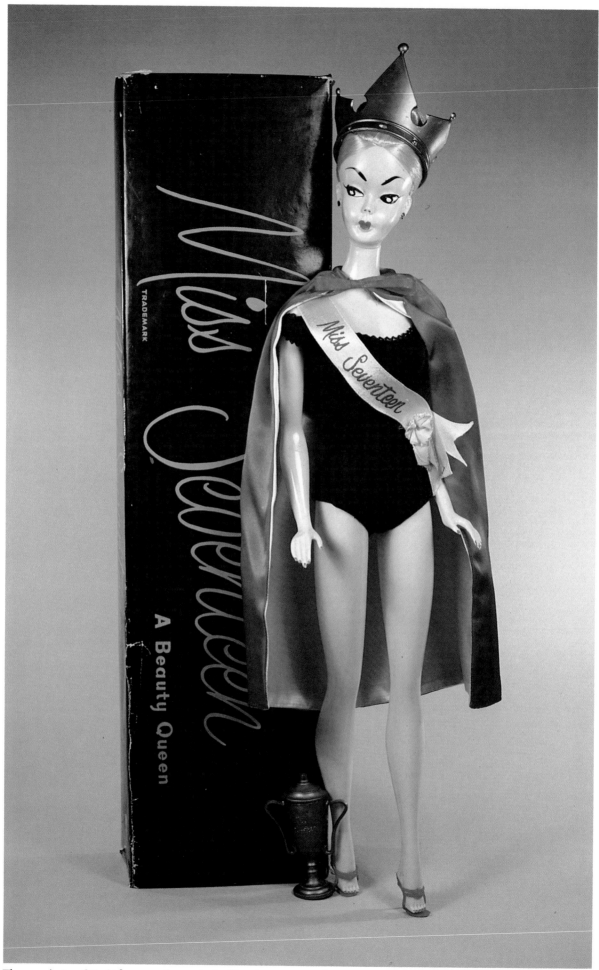

The popularity of *Barbie* spawned many look-alikes, *Miss Seventeen, A Beauty Queen* being one of them. Issued in 1961 by Marx Toys, the doll was available in the shown 18in (46cm) size as well as a rarer 15in (38cm) version.

The Virga doll was a *Ginny*® knock-off of the 1950s.

The popularity of television's "American Bandstand" saw the show's host, Dick Clark, in an amusing autograph doll. Fortunately, this particular doll was not autographed by many a child's friend.

Ginny® is a registered trademark of Vogue Dolls, Inc.
Barbie® is a registered trademark of Mattel, Inc.
Miss Seventeen, A Beauty Queen® is a registered trademark of Marx Toys.

Platter Puss,® issued in 1959 by the Merrimac Toy Co., was the "official autograph mascot" for "American Bandstand." Like the *Dick Clark* doll, *Platter Puss* is ready and willing to be written on! *Teresa Carpinello Collection.*

Sweetie Doll® by Elite Creations was a generic version of the popular *Sandra Sue*® doll. *Teresa Carpinello Collection.*

Platter Puss® is a registered trademark of Merrimac Toy Co.
Sweetie Doll® is a registered trademark of Elite Creations.
Sandra Sue® is a registered trademark of Richwood Toys.

Casper, The Friendly Ghost® by Mattel and *Wendy, The Good Little Witch*® by Gund. *Teresa Carpinello Collection.*

Ballerina dolls were popular among the female baby boomers. The Capezio version is shown here. *Teresa Carpinello Collection.*

Arranbee Doll Company produced many high quality hard plastic dolls, among them the popular *Nanette*® issued from 1953 to 1958 in assorted costumes and hairstyles.

The *Nancy Ann Style Show*® doll by Nancy Ann, a beautiful mid 1950s hard plastic doll.

An exquisite hard plastic doll
from the Royal Doll Co.

Posy Pixi® by Vogue Doll Co. along with a plush *Rin Tin Tin. Teresa Carpinello Collection.*

Posy Pixi® is a registered trademark of Vogue Dolls, Inc.

The *Candy Fashion*® doll by the Deluxe Reading Co. was a beautiful *Revlon*®-type fashion doll available in supermarkets.

Candy Fashion® is a registered trademark of the Deluxe Reading Co.
Revlon® is a registered trademark of Revlon, Inc.

The cover lid of *Candy Fashion's*® box.

The popular trolls and the troll-like animals from the mid 1960s. *Teresa Carpinello Collection.*

Elsie, the Cow® from Borden Milk fame. *Teresa Carpinello Collection.*

The all-vinyl *Charlie Brown*® ensemble from 1958 by United Features Syndicate. *Teresa Carpinello
Collection.*

Mama and baby as portrayed by
Ideal's *Posy*® and American Charac-
ter's *Tiny Tears.*® *Teresa Carpinello
Collection.*

Two generic toddler dolls play chef at a stove by Marx Toys.

Part Three...

The Real Baby Boomers...

The Mandevilles

Most Christmas cards of the peri[...]
featured the children of the fami[...]
Here is the Mandeville family ca[...]
with the author shown on *Ponyp[...]*
1949.

What was Christmas without the yearly trip to the nearest large department store. For me, that meant John Wanamakers in Philadelphia. Here four-year-old Glenn looks at the camera instead of Santa, but made sure Santa knew what he wanted before his time was up!

The expression "a picture is worth a thousand words" was never truer than when used to describe the life of the luckiest generation! As the illustrations in this chapter show, the life portrayed on the early television sitcoms was based on reality for many. These pictures show the love these parents had for their children, the joy that dolls brought to the child and finally, they show a glimpse of a time when "class" meant care and loving instead of a designer's logo on a shirt.

Those viewing these pictures will have varied reactions. Those raised in the generations before will perhaps be jealous, for the baby boomers were born into a world free from war and depression and full of hopes and dreams. The people born of the boom generation may look at these pictures and fondly remember the love and care that was showered upon them for no other reason than that they existed. This generation was "unnecessary." Technology made children a luxury item in the boom years, instead of more field hands as in the days of the 1920s. Like any luxury item, they were handled carefully, coiffed to perfection and dressed daily like children today only dress for Easter Sunday. To the viewer born late in the 1960s and beyond, these photographs seem like a mystery, for many today in the world of disposable everything see no point in the life style these pictures represent. In our modern world, "play" clothes are the same as "day" clothes...Sunday is just another day to call out for a pizza and for many, toys are merely a diversion between television shows.

Perhaps the truth can be found somewhere in the middle of all three of these views. Life in the boom years was for many a Disneyesque fantasy, fine if you liked your destiny planned for you, and in rhythm with the morals and values of the period. There were fewer choices. Little girls grew up to be brides and little boys worked to support them. A woman was a nurse and a boy was a doctor. The rules were simple and if you were content with them, the brass ring could be yours.

Today our world is better in many ways. As a man, I can be a doll collector and my female friends can be great doctors. The rules are all different. The cowboy in the white hat does not always win because the one in the black hat does not fight fair. Because today there are no rules, those of us raised with nothing but them often find confusion and frustration as we sadly learn that many of the values we were taught as a child no longer apply if one is to survive. The word "loyalty," whether to a job, a company (or a company to you), a spouse or a child, seems to be a forgotten word.

Yet hope looms on the horizon. Many of the baby boomers are looking back to their childhood and realizing that many things that were lost along the way DO still have meaning. Out of this is coming a "back to basics" movement, reflected in the doll industry today, that says let us combine the freedom of the 1990s with some of the old fashioned security and loyalty of the 1950s. The fondness that my generation has for their childhood and the fervor with which they collect the dolls they loved, lost or never had, is unexplainable to many.

To myself, the future offers hope to the children born of today that they may have the sense to recognize what is valid from the past and what is invalid in today's world and strike the happy balance that has been missing for some time now.

Perhaps many of us, too young at the time to see beyond the wide screen of Cinemascope or the animation of Walt Disney, wear rose-colored glasses about the past.

For doll collectors, the golden age of doll making in the 1950s and 1960s showed American technology at its finest. Not since the French bébés of the 1880s had quality been available to so many for so little.

Come glance now at pictures of the REAL baby boomers and beside them, the professional models of catalogs of the period. See for yourself how much was real and how much was hype. In the eyes of these children can be seen the trust, the love and the promise they believed was there.

This was not only the Golden Age of Collectible Dolls, but the golden age of youth as well. A world made of hope, love and the "American Dream."

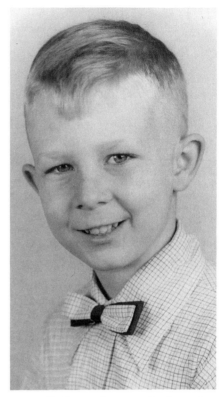

By first grade at age six, the author looked like Howdy Doody but at the time, that was not a bad image to have! Note the matching bow tie and shirt of baby boom perfection!

Mary Kamp Senne, the epitome of a true "baby boomer," shown here at age three with her *Tiny Tears* doll that she named "Dovey." This professional photograph was taken November 21, 1951, and carries the spirit of a child forever!

Tiny Tears® is a registered trademark of the American Character Doll Corp.

134

Who says boys cannot have dolls too? David Meisinger happily flaunts his "David" doll of 1953.

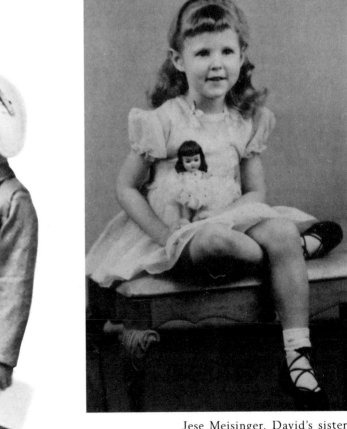

Jese Meisinger, David's sister, proudly sits holding her *Ginny*® doll in 1953.

Ginny® is a registered trademark of the Vogue Doll Company.

Greetings

Lois   PEGGY

Back in the "old" days families sent personal Christmas cards showcasing their members as in this greeting card from the Teaford family. This 1948 photograph preserves a magic moment with Lois and Peggy Teaford clutching their dolls. Lois holds "Bitsy" while Peggy clutches "Ma Butch."

The popular *Tiny Tears*® doll is held proudly by its owner, Geraldine Taylor, in 1958.

Tiny Tears® is a registered trademark of the American Character Doll Corp.

Ten-year-old Gidget Donnelly holds her lavishly dressed bride doll while sister Connie clutches her baby doll and brothers Ed and Clyde strum away on the "Santa given" guitars! It looks like it was a happy Christmas.

The *Penny Brite*® doll was a big hit in the early 1960s, especially with sisters Julie (Perez) and Betsy (Bieler). Notice the happy smile on Julie's face as she holds her formally dressed *Penny Brite*® in white!

Who says you can never have enough dolls? Six-year-old Diane Kornhauser smiles smugly at the camera in 1956 surrounded by many of her favorite dolls. Can you name them all?

Penny Brite® is a registered trademark of the Deluxe Reading Corp.

Cookie Pruit, alias Ruth Sharon Leif, reads her twin dollies a Christmas story as she smiles happily for the camera. Notice the beautiful seated *Toni* doll.

Toni is a registered trademark of The Gillette Co.

138

Caught in a moment of play, Teresa Carpinello smiles sheepisly for the camera while holding her *Revlon*-type doll. I love the rolled jeans!

Eight-year-old Nancy Mills Farley sits proudly, displaying her doll and bear collection. Now "40," she still has most of the items shown...a true baby boomer!

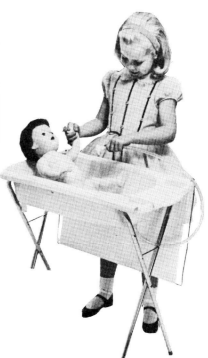

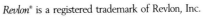

Revlon® is a registered trademark of Revlon, Inc.

139

Avid *Barbie*® collector Susan Miller showcases Santa's gift to her for Christmas 1962, *Barbie's Dream House.* As Susan wrote, "I felt like the luckest girl in the world."

One of the last of the baby boomers, two-year-old Dick Tahsin takes a ride with Great Grandma on his new three wheeler, Christmas 1966.

Barbie® is a registered trademark of the Mattel, Inc.

Bibliography

Bronson, Fred. *The Billboard Book of Number One Hits*. N.Y.: Billboard Publications, Inc., 1985.

Brooks, Tim. *The Complete Directory to Prime Time TV Stars*. N.Y.: Ballantine Books, 1987.

Edelstein, Andrew J. *The Pop Sixties*. N.Y.: World Almanac Publications, 1985.

Halliwell, Leslie. *Halliwell's Film Guide, 5th Edition*. N.Y.: Charles Scribner's Sons, 1980.

Hine, Thomas. *Populuxe*. NY: Albert A. Knopf, 1987.

Mandeville, A. Glenn. *Doll Fashion Anthology and Price Guide*. Cumberland, Md.: Hobby House Press, Inc., 1987.

_____ *Ginny...An American Toddler Doll*. Cumberland, Md.: Hobby House Press, Inc., 1985.

McNeil, Alex. *Total Television*. N.Y.: Penguin Books, 1980.

Smith, Patricia. *Modern Collector's Dolls*. Paducah, Ky.: Collector Books, 1973.

Index